HOW TO
BREAK
100

HOW TO BREAK 100

Golfing shortcuts
the pros don't teach you

Steve Mucha with Peter Mucha
Illustrations by David Wool

WALKER AND COMPANY
NEW YORK

Mucha, Steve.
  How to break 100.
    1. Golf.   I. Mucha, Peter.   II. Title.   III. Title: How to break
one hundred.
GV965.M72 1981   796.352'3   81-51967
ISBN 0-8027-0693-2   AACR2
ISBN 0-8027-7182-3 (pbk.)

First published in the United States of America in 1982 by the Walker
Publishing Company, Inc.

Published simultaneously in Canada by John Wiley & Sons Canada,
Limited, Rexdale, Ontario.

ISBN: 0-8027-0693-2 (cloth)
        0-8027-7182-3 (paper)

Library of Congress Catalog Card Number: 81-51967

Printed in the United States of America

10 9 8 7 6 5 4 3 2 1

Contents

AUTHOR'S FOREWORD

For more than twenty years, Steve Mucha tried to break 100 in golf. He took lessons from the pros. He listened to the advice of friends. He read lots of articles and books. He bought better equipment. But he still couldn't break 100.

At one point he was ready to give up the game. He said it was "downright embarrassing" to score so high in front of other golfers.

Then one day, after thinking about all the well-meaning advice he'd been given, Mucha made a simple discovery about how to make solid contact on almost every shot. The first day he tried out his new-found technique, he shot 20 strokes below his average. Soon afterwards, for the first time in his life, he won a trophy in a local golf league—then went on to win eight more in just two years. Now he regularly shoots in the mid-80's on some very tough courses.

Since making his discovery Mucha has shown his simple system to over 150 high-average golfers, and most of them drastically reduced their scores immediately. This experience has taught him that the pros don't necessarily have the best answers for the golfer struggling just to break 100.

In this book Mucha not only explains his simple system for making consistent contact, he also offers many shot-saving shortcuts that he's discovered during more than thirty years as an avid weekend golfer. All his tips and suggestions are specifically tailored for the high-average golfer who may be struggling to break 100 for the first time but who doesn't have all the time in the world to practice.

His son, Peter, who helped in the writing of this book, is a professional journalist who has written regularly for *The Philadelphia Inquirer* and has been published in *The New York Times*. Peter, who first learned to play golf from his father, consistently shot in the 80's while in high school.

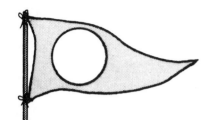

Introduction:
How to
cut your score
quickly
and easily

If you've been trying unsuccess-
fully to average under 100 but nothing seems to
work, what should you do? The only answer,
according to the pros, is to master the mechanics of the swing and then practice, practice,
practice. Take lessons from a pro or read lots of
books and articles written by the pros, then play
and practice constantly to master the funda-
mentals. That's the method the pros promote.

Unfortunately, huge numbers of golfers don't
have the time, the money, or the motivation to
benefit by this advice. They're too busy, too tired,
too lazy, or just plain too sensible to spend their
evenings and weekends stooping over rubber
tees at driving ranges or slapping plastic golf
balls around in the back yard. Oh, sometimes, in
desperation or sheer naiveté, they'll take a

lesson or two from a pro, hoping that a little help is better than none at all. The truth is, however, that without lots of practice to help the pro's suggestions sink in, a lesson is at best a waste of time. In fact, it can even make things worse.

After all, what usually happens when a duffer takes a single lesson? You ought to know, because it's probably happened to one of your friends, if not to you. The pro tells his student dozens of things that are wrong with his grip, his stance, and his swing. Then the student, trying to get his money's worth, struggles to master them all in one afternoon. Somehow, he actually does manage to twist his hands into that "better" grip. Somehow, he actually manages to swing the club in that "proper" way. And somehow he even manages to hit a couple of shots long and straight. On the driving range. Excited, the student can't wait to get out on the course. And when he does, he even remembers forty-five out of the fifty rules the pro told him. For the first three holes. Then it all falls apart. He starts topping and flubbing again, and he can't even regain his old comfortable swing. He shoots worse than ever, which makes him angry. Then he realizes he's thrown away twenty bucks, which makes him even angrier.

But it could have been worse. Pity the poor guy who took a lesson yesterday. The pro suggested to him that it might help to buy a whole new set of clubs.

There must be a better way—a way better

suited to the needs of the high-average golfer who doesn't have much time to practice. There must be a way for the high-average golfer to lower his score without investing lots of hours and dollars.

Fortunately, there is. And that's what this book is about. Believe it or not, it is possible to average under 100—or even under 90—without overhauling your swing, without memorizing a lot of complicated rules, and without hours and hours of practice. You really don't need a flawless grip, a sensational stance, fancy equipment, or a great physique to break 100. And you don't even need an expert understanding of the mechanics of the swing.

What you do need is sound advice for making the most of the skills you have right now. You see, the pro's advice is difficult to master without practice because it involves changing your swing and learning new skills. Developing significantly better habits does require a lot of practice. If you're out to break 80, improving your skills makes a lot of sense, but it's just plain unnecessary if all you want is to average under 100. It's therapeutic overkill, like having brain surgery to cure a simple headache. The truth is that if you're averaging over 100, there are a great many places you can cut strokes off your game without working to better your swing.

Just take the problem of failing to hit the ball squarely, a problem that plagues a great many high-average golfers, costing them countless strokes. In fact, chopping and topping the ball are such serious faults that many golfers could break 100 tomorrow if they could remedy just this one frustrating problem. The pros would tell you there's only one solution: Revamp your swing and practice so that you can hit the ball dependably when you're in the proper relation to it. But that's completely unnecessary! Chapter One of this book will show you how to make solid contact almost every time, even if your swing is lousy and you are standing in the "wrong" place. The suggested technique is so simple you can master it in minutes, saving yourself untold time, money, aggravation, and strokes.

Or take the problem of never being sure how far or in what direction your shots are going to travel. Again, the pros would show you the "right" swing and tell you to practice. Chapter Two will show you instead how to get more control and consistency *out of the same basic swing you've always used*, while explaining the surprising truth that for occasional players, bad habits are better than no habits at all. Or take the problem of hitting crooked tee shots. The pros would try to get you to eliminate all the "flaws" in your swing. They might even show you a trick that could work—for a while. Chapter Three will show you instead how to live with your hook or slice if you can, and the most sensible way to correct it if you can't. And there's no jabber about hips and knees and shoulder turns.

The rest of the book follows suit. Chapter Four will point out which shots you need to lower your score, and which shots you don't. It will show you how to get more out of your game by actually using fewer clubs. Chapter Five will demonstrate how to think your way to a lower score, by putting a little more savvy in your strategy and by avoiding those dreaded penalty strokes. Finally, Chapter Six will show you how to coax the maximum possible benefit out of any little bit of practicing you might choose to do. By the time you've finished taking in the sights on this six-stop tour, you'll be well on your way to making the utmost of your abilities. Your swing will still basically be the same, and your head won't feel crammed with technical bits of advice. But your score, ah, your score, that will never be the same again.

How to master solid contact in minutes

If you frequently top your Titleist or drive your divots farther that your Dunlop, you're obviously not making proper contact. What's the cure? A major overhaul of your swing, the pros will tell you. Keep your head still, bend those knees a little more, straighten that back a bit, left arm straight, lift your hands some, no that's too much, turn your hips, don't push them, follow through—and forty other things to remember. Including, "Relax!" You practice this advice a little, then you try to remember all of it when you go back out on the course. What happens? More digging and denting, what else? Yet there is a way to make consistent solid contact—a way that is so simple and so effective it only takes minutes to master and could cut a dozen strokes off your game the first day you try it. The pros won't tell you about it. I had to discover it for myself.

One day ten years ago, while I was warming up to play and wondering why I frequently made poor contact, I suddenly had an idea for a new technique. It seemed perfectly natural and logical, so I tried using it that day. Now, at that time, although I'd been trying to break 100 for many years (I'd even have been satisfied to shoot 99-7/8), I was still averaging about 112. Well, the day I tried this new technique I shot an 88 on a 6,300-yard course. I was so excited I played again the next day—and I shot another 88.

I couldn't believe what was happening. I'd been struggling for years to shave a stroke here, save a stroke there, and suddenly my score dropped more than 20 points! A friend of mine laughed when I told him about it, but when he tried it that day he also took 20 strokes off his game.

Since that day I have shown this technique to more than 150 golfers, and the results have been nothing less than astonishing. Four out of every five immediately reduced their scores tremendously. Of twenty, for example, who were averaging about 105, ten started shooting in the 90s, and ten skipped the 90s and started scoring in the 80s. Of twenty who were averaging about 120, fifteen promptly started breaking 100. One beginner who had never even broken 140 even went out and shot a 103.

The idea was very simple. It didn't involve any elaborate "mechanics" or any intricate knowledge of the "right" way to swing. When the pros try to teach you to make better contact, they tell you the ideal place to stand in relation to the ball, then they teach you the ideal way to swing accordingly. This approach is fine if you have the patience and dedication to practice and perfect such an ideal swing, but if you don't it's a frustrating disaster. So why not, I thought, just let the position of the ball fit the individual swing, instead of forcing the swing to fit some ideal ball position. Each individual swing must have a different spot for making the best contact, I reasoned, so all that is needed is a method for finding that best contact spot for each individual swing. And that's how I came up with the technique I call the *Check-it Swing*. Since this technique skirts all those complicated rules about the proper way to swing, it's so simple that it can be explained briefly and mastered quickly. Rarely have I needed more that two minutes to demonstrate this simple technique to anyone.

Select the club for the shot you're going to make, then step backwards away from the ball and take a Check-it practice swing. Imagine you are actually hitting the ball, taking a normal, natural swing while making sure to cut through the grass as close to the ground as you can without taking a divot. Let me emphasize that. *Cut through the grass as low as you can without taking a divot.* Now, carefully notice the area where the grass is clipped. That's where the bottom of your swing is, so that's where the ball has to be for your individual swing. Now step forward, making sure that your stance is in the right relationship to the ball. If you look carefully you'll probably notice that the ball may be several inches away from the position in which you're used to addressing it. If it is, then that's the reason for all your frequent mis-hits. The ball simply wasn't positioned at the bottom of your swing. So in this new position, take the same normal swing you took on your Check-it practice swing, again being sure to cut the grass off at the dirt. As long as you duplicate the swing and as long as you stand in the same relative position to the ball, you should make solid contact.

But you must do your best to duplicate your position relative to the ball. If you stand too far forward you'll top the ball. If you stand too far behind you'll hit dirt. If you stand farther away or up straighter, you could also top the ball. If you stand too close or bend forward too much, you could clunk it off the heel of the clubhead.

To be more specific, however, that clipped area may be several inches long and a couple of inches wide. Exactly where in that area should the ball be? The general rule is: The longer the club, the closer the ball should be to the middle of the clipped area. For long irons and fairway woods (if you can use these clubs reliably), the ball should be right in the middle, at the very bottom of your swing. For short irons—the 7, 8, 9 and pitching wedge—place the ball at the back or beginning of the clipped area, or about three inches before the middle. That's it—two basic fairway ball positions. The ball should be at the very bottom of your swing for long clubs and three inches before the bottom for short clubs.

The Check-it swing will also help you with tee shots. In this case, you should stand so that the tee is a few inches in front of the middle of

1. BALL PLACEMENT PRINCIPLES

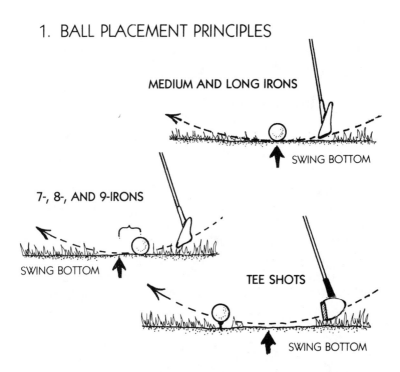

MEDIUM AND LONG IRONS

SWING BOTTOM

7-, 8-, AND 9-IRONS

SWING BOTTOM

TEE SHOTS

SWING BOTTOM

the clipped area. The exact spot will depend upon how high you tee the ball. Get in the habit of teeing the ball the same height every time so that you can learn what location works best for you. These placement principles are illustrated in Figure 1.

The reason that the ball should be behind the bottom of the swing for shorter irons is that these clubs have more sharply angled clubfaces. The arc of the swing with a short club is also sharper. As a result, shorter clubs dig into the ground faster than longer ones. With longer clubs, the clubface is less sharply angled and the arc of the swing is flatter, so they tend to dig into the ground less quickly. In other words, the shorter the club, the more careful you have to be to hit the ball *before you hit the ground.*

Some high-average golfers apparently don't believe that you should hit the ball before you hit the ground. One day I was playing with a building contractor who was 6-foot-3-inches tall, weighed 225 pounds, and could hit 280-yard tee shots. In all directions. His second shots weren't very good either, but he still somehow managed to get within 100 yards of the green in 2 on long par 4s. After watching him score 7s on the first two holes, I asked him why a big fellow like him was using a full-swing 7-iron from only 80 yards out. His reply was, "I don't get much distance because I can't seem to hit the ground right." Then he stood up to the ball and swung. This time he hit the ball before he hit the ground. It sailed 150 yards, over the green and into the trees. One stroke to chip out, one stroke to chip on, and two putts gave him another 7.

At this point I explained to him how to Check-it for the short irons. He gave me a funny look. "But I thought the divot was *under* the ball, not after it," he said. "Who told you that?" I asked. "Nobody. I just figured it out for myself," he replied. I explained to him that the only way to make solid contact is to make sure that the clubface hits the middle of the ball. If the clubface hits dirt first, then the dirt will get between the ball and the clubface and the ball will go nowhere. "Maybe I should just try to skim through the grass and try to scoop the ball off the ground," he suggested. "No," I explained. "If you skim through the grass, you'll top the ball. The clubface won't be low enough to meet the center of the ball. And scooping is too difficult," I added. "No, don't be afraid of taking a little dirt with your irons. Just make sure that you hit the ball first. That's the best way to make proper contact." Using Check-it, Joe didn't miss another green from 125 yards out all day, and he broke 100 for the first time in several years. In fact, he shot an 89.

Over the years I've noticed that a great many high-average golfers make some of these same wrong assumptions. They hit the ground before the ball, or they don't swing low enough to get a solid hit. Unfortunately, many of them continually worry about correcting the "defects" in their swings, when a little common sense about making solid contact is really all they need.

Okay, once you've found the spot where you make best contact with a particular club, you should remember that spot for the rest of the day, right? Wrong! It is vital to realize the following fact: Every single shot you take is unique, one of a kind. *Therefore, it is important to Check-it before every single shot.* The spot for best contact will change constantly, if only slightly, because of many factors. The way the spot varies with length of the club has already been mentioned. The slope of the ground is also an important factor. Even on a moderate downhill lie, for example, your downswing is likely to hit the ground several inches before it would on flat ground. On an uphill lie, the opposite is true. Since the slope is constantly changing, that's one reason to Check-it every time. The spot for best

2. SOLID CONTACT PRINCIPLES

**SKIM THE GRASS AND
YOU'LL TOP THE BALL**

**HIT THE DIRT FIRST AND
YOU'LL HAVE A WEAK HIT**

**HIT BALL, THEN GROUND,
AND YOU'LL MAKE
SOLID CONTACT**

contact also depends on how good your lie is, how thick the grass you're standing on is, your overall mood, and even your attitude about a particular shot. Also, at the start of each round you swing differently than you do after you've warmed up for a while. And by the end of the round,when you're feeling tired, you'll be swinging in still a different way. All these factors vary from one shot to the next, making the spot for best contact vary, too. So Check-it before every shot.

One day I was playing a tense match with a friend of mine. We had a tiring neck-and-neck battle all day, and at the end of 17 holes the score was tied. On the 18th, we both hit good tee shots that gave us good lies in the fairway. My oppo-

nent took a 3-wood and addressed the ball
where he'd been playing it all day, about even
with his left heel. He took a full swing and
topped the ball. It moved an inch. Then he
shifted his feet so that the ball was in the middle
of his stance, and this time the ball went 190
yards down the fairway.

I Checked-it and found the bottom of my
swing with a 3-wood had also shifted to the
center of my stance. I played it there and hit the
ball 180 yards. I won by one stroke, that stroke for
his shot that moved an inch. I'm sure that if I
hadn't checked my swing, I would have topped
my shot too. I've noticed over the years that
when you're nervous, the bottom of your swing
can move. It's at one spot when you're warming
up. It's at another after a couple of holes. And it's
at still another when you're tired or tense. That's
what happened to my opponent and me—we
got tense and, as a result, we weren't reaching
out and moving forward as freely on our swings.

Every shot you take is unique, one of a kind. In
fact, since your swing can vary so much, it's a
good idea not to wait too long between the
Check-it swing and the real thing. Try to hit your
shot within 20 seconds of Checking-it.

The amazing thing about the Check-it swing is
that it takes into account all of the following
factors, and does so automatically:

- Your individual swing
- Your individual stance
- Your individual grip
- The club you are using
- The slope of the ground

- The type of lie you have
- How warmed up you are
- How tired or tense you feel

Even with a flawless, picture-perfect swing, you'd have to do a lot of calculating and adjusting to account for all these factors unless you use the Check-it swing. So why spend lots of money on a pro? Why spend lots of hours practicing? Why revamp your swing? Why change your stance? Why worry about getting new equipment? Why remember lots of rules? Why should you do any of this when you have a simple technique that takes into account all sorts of factors and adjusts for them accordingly? As long as you can duplicate a swing from one minute to the next and as long as you can visualize where to stand in relation to the ball, you can solve your problem of nicking and topping and popping up golf balls. By using the Check-it swing, you should be able to eliminate many, many atrocious, horrendous, and costly mistakes. Before you know it, shots you once accepted as just mediocre, you'll be considering poor. If before, a bad 5-iron shot went 50 yards, now a disappointing one will travel at least 100. If before, a bad shot with a 3-wood went 70 yards, now a really rotten one will go 140.

Some big claims? You bet these are big claims. But don't just sit around thinking about them. Get out there and try out the Check-it swing the next time you play. Check-it before every shot, and see if you don't immediately start making better contact and cutting a lot of strokes off your score.

How to improve your control and consistency

The Check-it swing can cut many strokes off your score, and it may even be enough to help you accomplish your goal of averaging under 100. But it isn't the only thing you can do to lower your score without practice. After all, it can't correct everything. It won't help you hit the ball straight. It won't help you judge distances properly. And, of course, if your swing is so inconsistent that you can't duplicate the Check-it swing on the shot that counts, it won't help you at all. To tackle these problems, you're going to have to take the same basic swing you use now and make it more controlled, more consistent, more effective.

The recommendation of the pros would be to work on the mechanics of your swing and overhaul it. Learn to swing all over again. Grip like this, stand like that, turn just so. Remake the swing from top arc to bottom. Then they tell you to work on it until you get it right. But without lots of practice, it's nearly impossible for seasoned golfers to learn new tricks. So unless you're willing to practice for days and weeks until you get it right, an overhaul will just leave you frustrated, confused, and still scoring 110.

What's the solution? The solution is simple. In fact, the reason that most occasional golfers don't realize the solution, or are afraid to try it, is that it's too simple. It almost seems too obvious to bother emphasizing, but the keys to scoring well in golf are control and consistency. If you can't control your shots, you won't be able to achieve your goals, whether they are to stay in the fairway, stay out of a lake, or land on a green. And if you don't have consistency—if you can't control every shot and every type of shot to some degree—you're going to pile up a lot of unnecessary strokes on your way around the golf course. On the other hand, if you do have control and consistency, the Check-it swing will help you hit the ball squarely. If you have control and consistency, you can quickly learn to judge distances properly. With control and consistency you can learn to hit the ball straight or at least learn exactly how much to allow for your slice or hook. Control and consistency are therefore crucial to making the most of your present golfing abilities.

How do you develop control and consistency without practicing and practicing? The answers will seem almost too simple to believe. *Stop deliberately swinging out of control, and stop being deliberately inconsistent.* The fact is that almost all of the high-scoring golfers I've ever seen are their own worst enemies. They struggle so hard to improve, they actually make things worse.

They want more distance, so they swing harder. But swinging harder throws them off balance, causing them to lose control. Or they keep experimenting with different grips, stances, and swings in hopes of finding some magical arrangement that will solve all their problems. They don't realize that when you are a part-time player, using a swing that feels comfortable over and over is far more effective than struggling, straining, and experimenting, which robs you of any "feel" for your swings and costs you consistency. In fact, in golf it's actually better to have bad habits than no habits at all. If you consistently hook or slice, for example, you can probably compensate. But if you don't know whither your Wilson goest, all you can do is hit and pray.

Every professional athlete knows the importance of consistency. "Play within yourself" and "know your limitations" are familiar bits of advice to professionals in all sports. But too often amateurs don't realize that trying too hard can be disastrous. It costs you consistency and makes big mistakes more likely. If you try to serve an ace in tennis, you're more likely to fault. If you try to make a seven-ten-pin split in bowling, you're more likely to miss entirely than if your aims had been more modest. You're more likely to strike out if you aim for the fences than if you try for a solid single. Of course, if you're good at hitting home runs, maybe it's worth it to you to strike out a few more times, but if you're not that good, you're going to have to be a consistent singles hitter to stay in the major leagues.

Unfortunately, too many of the Ty Cobbs on the golf course think they're Babe Ruths. They take gigantic backswings. They lash the club at the ball. And they always attempt the improbable: cutting the dogleg, clearing the lake, or punching the ball out of the woods. Once in a while they hit a lucky bloop double, but more often they simply strike out, slicing the ball into the sycamores or duffing it into the drink. Some golfers apparently think that hitting an occasional spectacular shot is a sign they know what they're doing. On the contrary, the spectacle is more likely to indicate dumb luck or brute force rather than control.

Will the Check-it swing solve the erratic tendencies of these would-be home run hitters? Unfortunately not. Too many things can go wrong with a swing that's strained. The head can bob, the arms can twist, the body can lunge on one shot, then fall backwards on the next. You can't be consistent when you're out of control, and the Check-it swing can't help if you can't be consistent. You've got to "know your limitations" and "play within yourself." Don't try to swing as hard as a pro unless you practice as much as a pro. Stop deliberately swinging out of control. Whenever you press and try to play over your head, you're going to lose control and lose strokes. It's really that simple.

Besides, even the pros know the value of an easy swing. I've heard the following story many times, but it's worth repeating: Before a tournament a young amateur was practicing on the driving range with a 9-iron. On each shot he was taking a big backswing and hitting the ball far, but he was spraying the ball in all directions. An older teaching pro who was watching came up to him and said, "Shorten your backswing twenty-five percent and see if you don't hit the ball just about as far." When the young amateur tried this seventy-five-percent swing, his shots were straighter and he lost no distance at all. "Interesting, isn't it?" the old man said, smiling. "Swing easy to hit the ball far and straight."

Solid contact, you see, is the key to hitting the ball well, and control of the swing is the key to getting solid contact. Strength and backswing speed are not the crucial factors. Extra muscle can't help you if you can't convert it into solid contact, and, in fact, the speed of the backswing contributes absolutely nothing to hitting the ball farther. It can throw you off-balance, but it can't help you gain distance on your shots. With a slow backswing you can coil your muscles for the downswing just as well as you can with a fast backswing. The backswing does nothing but help you get ready for the all-important downswing, so don't let your backswing blow it. Take an easy backswing. With an easy swing you are more certain to hit the ball with control and consistency.

The same thing goes for backswing size. I used to believe in the "kill it with a big backswing" philosophy myself. I'd be satisfied with 100-yard wormburners and 150-yard barkbouncers in hopes that I'd make up for them later with a 225-yarder down the middle to brag about. But over the years I've come to realize that averaging 190 yards in the fairway is far better than spraying all over the course hoping for a big hit. One reason is that you get occasional big hits anyway. Years ago, when I was a duffer averaging 112, I was playing a hole with a lake 160 yards off the tee. You had to hit the ball 180 yards on the fly to clear the lake. For months I'd been plunking balls into the water, so on this occasion I decided to play it safe. Instead of my usual "kill-it backswing" with a 1-wood, I took an easy swing with my 4-iron. The ball cleared the water. I was dumbfounded. It was one of the longest 4-irons I ever hit. But I thought it was a fluke, so on the next hole I was back to my "kill-it backswing" for a 150-yard drive. I shot my usual 115 that day. But now I know better. Swing easily but firmly, and you'll get the best results. Don't try to swing like a pro unless you're willing to practice like a pro.

Once you've made up your mind to play within your limitations, you're well on your way to getting your swing under control. No more lunging or falling off balance. No more deliberately pulling or pushing the club wildly around.

And what's more, you'll probably find that your swing feels more comfortable and that you're making some better shots and fewer mistakes. Instead of swinging a tiger by the tail and believing you're in control, you'll be swinging a golf club.

Now, with your swing more under control you're ready to gain more consistency. The way to develop consistency without practice is to choose a swing you can count on and then get a feeling for that swing. The idea is to develop a style of swinging you can return to again and again. You do this in two basic ways. First, develop a comfortable rhythm to your swing so that you have a feeling you can come back to. Second, always use that style of swinging. Everywhere. When you play. If you practice. On the tee. In the fairway. Around the green. With plastic practice golf balls, real golf balls, or no golf balls at all. Depending on the club, some swings will have larger backswings than others, but they should all have the same basic rhythm, the same basic feel. Unless you're willing to take lessons and practice, abandon random experimentation. Give up being deliberately inconsistent.

This is not to say that you need to develop a radically new swing. If you've been playing golf for a while, chances are the basic mechanics of your swing are good enough for you to shoot in the 90's, if you can only develop consistency. You've probably already ironed out any extremely serious technical problems with your swing, and you probably have a decent idea of what a good swing is. Even if you do have some technical "flaws," you've probably already found ways to adjust for them so that you can hit the ball in the direction you want to. If this is the case and if you have decided to play within your limitations, you don't need a new swing, you just need more rhythm in the old one. By putting more rhythm in your swing, you'll develop a feel for that swing, a feeling that lets you know whether one swing is like the next. The goal is to make all your swings alike enough to develop control over every one of them. Just as by developing control you develop consistency, so by gaining consistency you gain control. Helping one helps the other, and it puts you into a cycle of steady improvement.

How do you develop a sense of rhythm? It's very difficult, if not impossible, to teach. If you're lucky you just naturally know what rhythm is, when you have it and when you don't. But many of us need a few pointers, a few suggestions. First of all, what is rhythm? In golf, it's a sense of smoothness, of fluid motion, of controlled power. Jerking, straining, twisting, and stopping and starting are not parts of a rhythmical swing. Rhythm is also a sense of synchronization, of one thing following the next in a standard order, whatever the order is. If you sometimes start turning your hips before you start your downswing but other times start the downswing first, you don't have a good sense of rhythm. If sometimes you break your wrists before you hit the ball, sometimes as you hit it, and sometimes afterwards, you ain't got rhythm. Rhythm is also a sense of extension and speed. Your backswing may vary from club to club but every swing with a 5-iron, for example, should have roughly the same size backswing. And every swing should have roughly the same overall speed and the same speeds at different parts of the swing. The backswings should be similar speeds, and the clubhead should accelerate roughly the same way on every downswing. If the size and velocity of your swing are constantly changing, you haven't found your sense of rhythm. Perhaps more important, rhythm is also a sense of comfort. Your swing should feel comfortable to you, and it should feel effective. You don't want to be so relaxed you lose all power, but if your hands feel tight, your arms feel stiff, and your back feels strained, you're going to find it very difficult to use a particular swing constantly.

A word of caution, however. Rhythm is not swaying. Moving your body backwards on the wind-up and forwards on the swing is not the kind of rhythm you want in golf. Moving forward on the downswing does not add velocity to the ball; it throws your timing off. A good golf swing is a turning motion, not a swaying motion.

Next time you grab a golf club try to find your own comfortable swing. Using a wood is best because woods are longer and harder to swing. If you find your rhythm with a wood you should be able to use it on all your clubs. Just keep taking swings until you find a speed that feels comfortable and yet effective. A medium back-swing speed, for example, is probably best for the occasional golfer. A fast backswing is impossible to master and control, while a slow backswing feels uncomfortable and weak. The same advice applies to your downswing: Don't over-swing but don't swing without power. And, of course, always try to swing with the same clubhead speed from shot to shot. Get a sense of the size and speed of your swing as well as its unique synchronization and overall feel. It might help to use a combination of three words like "one-two-three" or "back-and-swing." When you pull the club away from the ball, say "back" to yourself. As you get near the top of your backswing, say "and." Then when you start your downswing, say "swing." The rhythm of the words will help you remember the rhythm of your swing.

Once you've found your swing, start using it all the time. Every time you use it you'll develop a better feel for it, and you'll be better able to tell when something starts to go wrong. Use it if you practice. Use it when you play. Don't experiment with faster swings on the driving range just to see how far you can hit a ball. Don't take harder tee shots to try to make up for a bad last hole. If you have to take a weaker swing (say you have to hit a weak 3-iron to get under a tree but not reach the lake), just make sure it's a smaller, slower version of your regular swing. Don't chop off some component like the backswing or the follow-through. It won't be possible to follow this advice all the time (sometimes it makes sense to punch a shot), but if you do your best, you'll be on your way towards getting the most out of all your clubs and all your shots. Even your putting stroke can be a miniature version of this same swing, but if it's not, don't worry about it. We've all seen a lot of strange putting styles that were very effective.

By following the advice in this chapter carefully, you should be able to transform what might have been an awkward, erratic motion into a controlled, consistent, comfortable swing. Although this swing may still have "flaws" in the eyes of the pros, it's a swing you can learn to use very effectively. Because it's consistent, you can quickly learn to become a better judge of distances. Because it's consistent, you can sidestep some of its defects more dependably with the Check-it swing. And because it's consistent, you'll soon have more confidence in predicting what direction the ball is going to travel. Then even if you still hook or slice, you'll be in a good position to compensate for the curving path of the ball. And that's the subject of the next chapter.

How to
hook or slice
and still survive

Many golfers worry persistently about not being able to hit the ball straight, and they struggle with their swings all day trying to hit one right down the middle. So they hook one, then slice one, then top one, and kick three. They're completely conditioned to the idea that you *should* hit tee shots straight as an arrow, and they anxiously dream about the day every shot travels in a line, not a curve.

For many golfers, the worry is needless. Just as you don't need fancy gloves or golf balls to score in the 90s, you don't need arrowline accuracy either. You just need to hit the ball in roughly the same manner most of the time. If you regularly slice somewhat, you can shoot 90. Even if you constantly hook moderately, you can break 100. All you need is consistency. That's one of the main reasons that so much attention was devoted to consistency in the last chapter: to help those golfers who suffer from trajectory trouble. After mis-hits, crooked shots are one of the occasional golfer's greatest problems. Fortunately, if the advice in the previous chapter has been carefully followed, consistency can be developed, and with consistency the problem of curving tee shots can be kept under control.

Once you have consistency, all you have to do—and you probably already know it—is to aim so that the curving flight of the ball carries it back into the fairway. It can be scary, because you'll occasionally hit one straight and end up in the woods or out-of-bounds. But, unless you're willing to take expensive lessons and practice extensively, this is the most sensible way. You'll be in the woods less often if you learn to trust your hook or slice than you will if you keep changing your swing and stance in hopes of discovering some magic key or correcting a vital flaw that will solve your problems forever.

You'll just have to accept that on holes that curve the wrong way (you slice but the hole doglegs left), you may have to use a shorter club and play it safe. Resist the temptation to try to hit straight. Don't worry, you can make up for it on the holes that bend in your favor. Unless you want to work hard to change your limitations, the thing to do is accept them and work with them. If you don't have the time to increase your skills through lots of lessons and practice, you have to make the most of skills you already possess. In the process you may even turn what seems like a liability into an asset. I have a friend, for example, whose tee shots are low, screaming slices. Not some of his tee shots, but all of them. And yet he rarely gets into trouble. Oh, his shots do come close to clunking the trees on the left and his ball does come close to rolling into the woods on the right, but he manages to be nearly immune from penalty strokes. And we play on a fairly narrow course, with thick pine trees lining each side of the fairway. So if you have a moderate slice or hook, don't worry about it. Live with it. Learn to make it work to your advantage. One of the nice things about having a natural fade or hook is that you actually get extra roll down the fairway. My friend averages just under 90.

But what if your slice is more accurately described as "wicked"? Or your hook more truthfully called "enormous"? What do you do? The first thing to do is review the last chapter and its advice about swinging smoothly and not swinging so hard. By swinging more rhythmically you may find that you'll start to hit the ball straighter. And by swinging less rapidly you'll at least find that the shorter the shot, the shorter the hook or the slice. Even if your 200-yard tee shots make sharp right turns, you'll probably discover that your 170-yard drives will slice only a medium amount. You can average under 100 with a 170-yard slight slice, but you can't with a 200-yard careening curveball, unless you play extremely wide-open courses. Even then, you might end up closer to the green by hitting the ball 170 yards in the right fairway instead of 200 into the next. So the next time you play try swinging more smoothly and cutting down on your swing. If it works, why not stick with it? Become a master of compensating, and stay out of trouble. You may lose a little distance off the tee, but you may also save quite a few strokes. And don't keep going back to the big whack to check if your problem somehow solved itself while you weren't looking. Even if it miraculously did, it could unsolve itself just as quickly.

If, however, trying to swing smoothly and cutting down on your swing don't seem to help, another remedy may be called for. You need to know a little bit about why shots curve in the first place. Simply, they curve because you're putting a spin on the ball. If, at the moment of impact, the clubface is facing off-line, the shot will be sent spinning. Or if your swing during impact is moving off-line, if it isn't moving directly towards the target, the shot will also loop away from the fairway. If both factors are out of kilter—clubface facing off-line, clubhead moving off-line—the result is an enormous hook or slice. (See illustration.)

The cure for your condition is fairly simple to describe. Make sure, at the moment of impact, that the clubface is facing the target and that the clubhead is traveling towards it. Don't let the club twist in your hands. Don't push or pull the ball off-line. Hit the ball squarely, with the club moving towards the target, so that the ball doesn't spin. If you can get a feel for keeping your swing, the clubface, and the target properly lined up as you hit the ball, you're well on your way towards getting your shots under control, if not towards hitting the ball straight.

Since this may be easier said than done, however, the following techniques may help you figure out what's causing your curving: The next time you're having trouble controlling your shots out on the course, try taking the same swing you've been taking, but this time stop the clubhead just before the spot where it would hit the ball. Look at the clubface. Does it face the target squarely? Try the swing a few more times just to check the results. If the clubface consistently faces off-line, you've found the source of your problem. Somewhere between your backswing and impact, the club is twisting or turning in your hands.

If, on the other hand, the clubface does face the target, you're probably moving the club off-line during impact. Concentrate on following through straight towards the target and see if your shots don't travel straighter.

That's it. That's all the advice you need to know to be well on your way to drastically reducing the problems you have with hooking or slicing. It may not be a cure-all, but it should help enough to cut back on both penalty shots and worrying. And you can achieve it without a lot of practice or monkeying around with the mechanics of your swing.

Since you probably won't be lugging this book around with you the next time you play, let's run through this advice one more time to help you remember it.

1) Develop a consistent swing by following the advice in Chapter 2: Get your swing under control, develop a rhythm in it and use that same rhythmical, comfortable swing all the time.

2) If your consistent swing leaves you with a moderate slice or hook, don't worry, compensate. Aim to allow for the curving flight of the ball.

3) If your slice or hook is gigantic, the first things to try are swinging more smoothly and swinging less hard. Test this advice the next time you play.

4) If after cutting down your swing, however, your shots are still uncontrollable benders, try to find out the cause of your curves. Take your regular swing, but stop the club in a position just before it would hit the ball. Is the clubface facing away from the target? Then work on keeping the club from turning in your hands. Is the clubface facing properly? Then work on swinging through the ball straight towards the target. In either case, concentrate on swinging so that your swing, the clubface, and the target are all lined up properly at the moment of contact with the ball.

Get to it, and good luck!

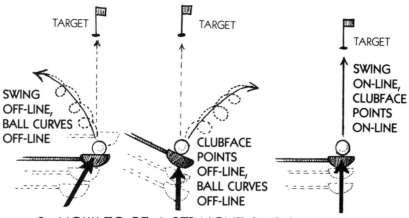

TARGET

TARGET

TARGET

SWING OFF-LINE, BALL CURVES OFF-LINE

CLUBFACE POINTS OFF-LINE, BALL CURVES OFF-LINE

SWING ON-LINE, CLUBFACE POINTS ON-LINE

3. HOW TO BE A STRAIGHT SHOOTER

How to select
the smartest
shots

One of the worst things a beginning golfer can do is watch the pros on TV. The pros are incredible! They crunch 270-yard drives straight down the fairway. They hit long irons out of the traps. They loft pitching wedges 130 yards right onto the green, with the ball rolling gently backwards toward the hole. They hit 2-irons 200 yards from a bad lie to within 20 feet of the flag. They even hit greens with fairway woods. They blast out of sandtraps to within a few feet of the flagstick, and they can deliberately fade or hook around doglegs. They shoot for the green even when they can't see it. Now isn't that the way to play golf? Aren't those the shots that everybody should try to make?

No, no, no, no, no. Those shots are not for every-other-weekend golfers who average 115.

They're not even for every-weekend golfers who average 95. Let's be realistic. Most golfers can't make half of those shots half of the time. I can't hit any of them. And I average 88.

Golf is a very different game for average and below-average players than it is for the pros. What gets results for one invites disaster for the other. It's like a child trying to run before he really knows how to walk. He can cover a lot of territory when he just concentrates on walking. But if he tries to sprint before he's ready, he'll fall, getting nowhere. In the same manner, the occasional golfer has to learn to master the simple shots first and then work his way up to the tough ones. But if he tackles the tough ones prematurely, he's bound to make a lot of mistakes, and his score will suffer as a consequence. Furthermore, every time he tries to hit like a pro, he misses an opportunity to develop greater control over the simple shots. Just think of other occasional golfers you know who attempt the most difficult shots. Have they mastered the simple ones? Of all those who attempt to hit 2-irons, can any consistently hit a 5-iron 150 yards? Of all those who try to pop pitch shots onto the putting surface, can any even regularly bounce the ball on with an easy 7-iron? Of all the players you know who hit 1-woods off the tee, how many can even count on being in the fairway when they hit a 3-wood or even a 3-iron instead?

Chances are not many, if any. In fact, it's probably easier for a golfer to break 100 without a driver, a 2-iron, or a pitching wedge than it is with them. If you average 89 and want to average 70, you'll need these clubs. But, if you're averaging 109 and you'd like to shoot 99 and love to score 94, you're probably better off without them. It's easier to control a 3-wood off the tee than a 1-wood. It's easier to hit a 4-iron from the fairway than a 2-iron. It's easier to master the chip-and-run than it is to master the pitch shot. So unless you have already mastered these clubs, or unless you are willing to practice until you can, stick with the clubs that are easiest to use. They're the least likely to get you into trouble. Besides, by reducing the number of clubs you use, you'll have fewer to learn to control, and each playing round will become a better practice session. By using clubs you can control, swinging smoothly, and concentrating on making good contact, you'll soon find you're making fewer costly errors. In fact, I know a golfer who recently broke 100 for the first time in his life, and he only used his 5-, 7-, and 9-irons and a putter.

The point is that the high-average golfer can help lower his score by selecting shots and clubs that are well-suited to his needs and abilities. Since his needs and abilities aren't the same as those of the touring pros, his repertoire shouldn't be the same either. Now when the pros choose their bag of tricks, they choose any shots that have the potential to be effective. Then they spend whatever time it takes to master those shots. On the other hand, the high-average golfer who doesn't have much time to practice has to go about things in the opposite way. He has to start with whatever is already reliable and then try to make it more effective. He has to concentrate on what he can already control. So, unless he's willing to dedicate enormous amounts of time to practice, the occasional golfer's repertoire has to consist of three basic types of shots: shots he can control, shots anybody can control, and shots that keep him out of trouble. For simplicity's sake, let's call them strength shots, simple shots, and safe shots. Let's discuss them one at a time.

Strength Shots. A strength shot is any shot you can execute reliably, no matter how difficult it is for other people to perform. Anything you do well on the golf course you should continue to do. If you use a driver well, use it. If you pitch like a pro, pitch. If you hit 2-irons well, then two's your lucky number. If you can hit fairway woods, or fade around doglegs deliberately, or hit long irons out of fairway bunkers, by all means do it.

Simple Shots. Unfortunately, most of us have very few, if any, strength shots. Therefore, we have to make the most of the simple shots, the shots that are easiest to master: the 3-wood tee shot, the fairway 5-iron, the chip-and-run approach to the green. Also included in this category is that deceptively simple shot, the putt.

Many occasional golfers, however, aren't even skillful with the chip-and-run. But approach shots to the green are so important that every occasional golfer who's serious about scoring well should use this shot and master it. The chip-and-run is basically a soft shot with a 7-, 8-, or 9-iron, in which the ball flies about two-thirds of the way to the green, then bounces and rolls the last third. It sounds simple, and it is easier to execute than the pitch shot. But the chip can present problems. One reason is that it's hard to get a feel for such a soft swing. It's hard to know just how hard to swing to hit the ball just so far. If you already have a good feel for chip shots, you're lucky. Whatever you're doing, stick with it. But if you don't, I recommend that you try a "stiff wrist" chip. Chip with a short backswing, zero wrist-action, practically no body turn, and a moderate follow-through. This swing will feel different from your usual swing, but it has several advantages. First, wrist-action is too hard to measure, to get a good feel for. So if you don't play all the time, you're not likely to know just how much flick to transmit to your Titleist. Using stiff wrists eliminates that variable. Second, body turn is also hard to gauge, and it introduces a lot of unnecessary motion. You don't need a lot of turn to hit a ball less than 50 yards. Finally, by eliminating these other factors you can gauge distances by controlling the size of your backswing. The bigger the backswing, the farther the ball will go. The other factors don't come into play. You can learn with careful observation as you play or practice just how far a one-third, one-half, or two-thirds backswing will send the ball. Your one-third backswing, for example, might send the ball 15 yards in the air, while your half-swing sends it 25. Wouldn't it be convenient to know that every time you're 35 yards from the green, a half-swing will make the ball fly 25 yards and roll the rest of the way? Using this simple "stiff wrist" chip can save you a lot of guesswork and scoring grief around the green. And remember that moderate follow-through. Never punch a golf shot unless you have to (say, to keep the club from hitting a tree). You can't control shots that are punched instead of stroked smoothly.

While we're on the subject of chipping, what club do you use from the fringe? What club do you use when you're almost close enough to putt, but the grass is still too deep? Many golfers I know use nothing but a 9-iron or a putter once they're within 90 yards of the hole. But a 9-iron tends to pop the ball up from the fringe, making the shot hard to control. That's why on short fringe shots, a 7-iron is actually the better club to use. It's less-angled face more closely resembles a putter, so you get better control. Use a little stiff-wrist chip, letting the ball pop up just enough to get on the green and then roll the rest of the way to the hole.

Once you're on the green, you're faced with the apparently easy task of putting. No longer do you have to worry about how badly you slice, how deeply you divot, or how poorly you swing. Even people with quirky stances and swings can be good putters. And aiming really isn't that much of a problem—you just have to keep the clubface square to the direction you want the ball to roll and then swing in that direction.

But, as every occasional golfer knows, there's many a flub between the putt and the cup. The biggest problem is knowing how hard to hit the ball. Golfers who play and practice a great deal can usually rely on "feel" in judging how hard to hit a putt, but the occasional golfer really needs something more tangible to trust. The system I use depends less on "feel" than on the size of my backswing. It's not complicated, and it's very dependable. All you have to do is use a consistent, pendulum-like swing and pay careful attention to how long a backswing corresponds to how long a putt.

Whenever I play I start out with a couple of assumptions. I assume that a 5-inch backswing will send the ball 10 feet on a level putting surface, and that a 10-inch backswing will propel the ball 30 feet. If I find on the first hole or two that my putts are long or short, I'll readjust my thinking. If the greens are fast and the ball goes too far, I'll allow maybe 4 inches of backswing for 10-foot putts and 8 inches for 30-footers. Rarely do I find a green so thick that I need 6 inches of backswing for a 10-foot putt. Of course, in-between distances correspond to in-between backswings. So with greens where a 10-foot putt requires 5 inches of backswing, a 15-foot putt might need 6 inches and a 22-footer about 8 inches. If the distance is very short, like 5 feet, you'll find the backswing should be about 3 or 4 inches, no less. After all, a couple of inches of swing are needed just to get the clubhead in motion.

For uphill putts add an inch of backswing for

shorter putts, perhaps two inches on longer ones. For downhill putts subtract an inch of backswing on short putts, subtract two inches on longer ones. These guidelines work dependably except on very steep slopes.

Another putting pitfall is reading the break correctly. It's not easy to know how much a certain slope will cause a putt to curve. Indeed, sometimes it's hard to tell even the direction the putt will curve. Although the key to mastering breaking putts is practice, there are a couple of things the occasional golfer can do. One is to double-check your idea of which way the putt will break by looking at the shot from the other side of the hole. Often that second angle will show you something you missed. Another tip is to watch how other players' putts are breaking. Be especially careful to watch putts that have to travel a similar line to the hole as yours.

Safe Shots. The final section of the occasional golfer's repertoire includes what I call safe shots. They could also be called smart shots. These are the shots that anyone can do, that no one is impressed by, and yet that no golfer seriously trying to lower his score can do without. The play-it-short-of-the-lake shot. The safe-side-of-the-green shot. The out-of-the-trap-anyway-you-can-in-1 shot. Even the penalty-stroke-out-of-the-woods. The central themes are "Keep out of trouble" and "When you're in trouble, escape as quickly as possible." After all, trying to turn misfortune into good luck often leads to disaster. How many times have you tried to hit out of the woods, only to end up deeper in it? How often have you seen someone try to drive the lake, fail, then try to drive it again, only to lose one more Maxfli in the mud and algae? Strokes can pile up very quickly when you flirt with danger hoping to get lucky. So know your weaknesses and avoid them. If you know you have trouble getting height on the ball, don't try to go over trees. If you know you aren't accurate, don't shoot for the flagstick two feet behind the sand trap. Aim for the wide open part of the green. If you haven't mastered sand shots, don't try to hit woods or long irons out of fairway bunkers—just get out. Hit a 9-iron. Putt out. But above all get out.

Sand traps, of course, are especially unkind to the occasional golfer. You must have a way to get out of sand traps without piling up strokes. Some occasional golfers use a punch-shot. Some use a kind of scoop-shot, attempting to get under the ball and lift. And some even putt the ball out, a shot which can be surprisingly effective. If the lie is good give the ball a good whack with your putter. The ball gets enough spin to roll up and over some very steep lips. As long as the ball isn't buried and the lip isn't too steep, you can usually get out of a trap in one stroke with a putter-smack.

Unfortunately, none of these shots can be relied upon all the time. You can't punch a ball over a high lip. You can't scoop a ball out of a bad lie. And you probably can't putt out in either case. So what's the solution? There is no easy solution. You could try using a combination of shots: a punch-shot for poor lies, a scoop-shot for higher lips, and when the lie is bad and the lip is high, a punch-shot out of the side of the trap. A good chip from the fringe could make up for the lost shot out of the trap. But you're still going to punch some shots over greens and scoop some shots not quite high enough to get out. So, if you have to use a combination of shots, the best advice is the obvious: Be careful to stay out of traps in the first place.

Since staying completely out of traps is impossible, however, the best answer is to take the time and trouble to learn to hit a proper sand shot. At the outset of this book I said that nobody needs lessons from a pro, complicated advice, or constant practice to average in the 90s. That's true. You don't have to hit a proper sand shot to average 95. After all, you don't face buried lies or cliff-like lips every round. But if there is one area in which rules, practice, and even lessons can give the most peace of mind to the occasional golfer, that area is the sand shot. Unlike every other shot in golf there is no simple but completely reliable substitute. And no shot in golf can so easily waste an entire stroke. If you dribble a ball off the tee, at least you're 50 yards closer to the hole. But if you duff a sand shot you can roll right back where you started from.

It's because the sand shot is so crucial that I offer the following rules on how to hit a sand shot for those willing to take the time and trouble to benefit from them. I've made this advice as simple as I can, but benefiting by it will require some experimenting and practice. Even if you can't commit much time, however, you still should read this advice. You might be one of the lucky ones who will find the right stroke with just a few attempts out on the course.

Rule 1: A proper sand shot hits the sand, not the ball.

That's right. Unlike every other shot, the object in the sand shot is to hit the ground—in this case the sand—before you hit the ball. You let the sand behind and under the ball do the shoving instead of the clubhead. It's nearly impossible to hit the ball first anyway, so you have to have a shot that works by hitting the sand first. How else could you get out of buried lies?

Rule 2: The thinner the clubhead, the less sand you can take.

Not all clubheads have the same thickness Some are thicker than others, or, to put it another way, they have a bigger flange.

This difference is important, because the size of the flange will affect the amount of sand you can safely take with your shot. The thinner the clubhead—the smaller the flange—the faster the club will dig down into the sand and tend to "bite," or bury itself. So if you use a club with a thin clubface, like a 9-iron with a sharp bottom, you must be careful to hit the sand no more than an inch or two behind the ball. On the other hand, a club that has a fat flange will dig in more slowly, and is less likely to get buried in the sand, which would result in the ball's barely budging. A wedge with a fat flange can be extremely effective hitting several inches behind the ball.

Of course, with any club you have to experiment to find the right amount of sand to take if you hope to control your distance. But since a club with a fat flange is less likely to bury itself, you have more room for error. If you ever buy a new sand wedge, make sure it has a fat flange.

Rule 3: Always follow through.

Remember, you're not hitting the ball, you're hitting and lifting sand and the sand has to push the ball. So you have to keep pushing when the club hits the surface in order to provide enough force to get the ball on the green. Keep swinging right through the sand. You should end up with a very high follow-through. It should almost feel as if you're shoveling the ball out.

Rule 4: Keep your nose 4 inches in front of the ball.

You have to lean forward a little to make a good sand shot. The leaning is needed to give the clubface the proper angle and to help you follow through pulling enough sand. If you lean backwards the sand won't push the ball at the proper angle.

Bury your feet into the sand about an inch. The combination of playing the ball in the center of your stance, burying your feet an inch, and positioning your nose 4 inches in front of the ball will allow you to take the right divot of sand just under the ball.

With these four rules in mind you should be

able to develop an effective sand shot that works for you and your club. You should be able to discover by experimenting just how much sand to take and just how hard to swing. In general, it's better to take a hard swing with a lot of sand than a weak swing with a little sand. Don't be afraid of the strong swing. As long as you hit the sand first, you're going to have trouble sending the ball over the green.

By the way, this sand shot will roll a little, so you're going to have to learn to allow for it. A pro might be able to show you how to hit a sand shot that doesn't roll much, but it's a much harder shot to master.

So if you're serious about lowering your score, rectify your repertoire. Stick to anything you do with excellence and anything you can do with ease. Substitute for shots you don't need that are impossible to master without an abundance of practice. And, if you can, try to develop some proficiency with shots that might cause a lot of trouble, like approach shots and sand shots. A better bag of tricks can save a lot of costly strokes.

How to think your way to a lower score

Okay, put your clubs back in the bag. Sit down. Stretch out. Relax your muscles. And read. In this chapter, all the suggestions for lowering your score involve only one thing: thinking. No need to grip. No need to stand. No need to swing. And you don't have to drive to a practice thinking place. There's not a single suggestion in this chapter for practicing or playing to improve your physical skills. This chapter simply tries to show how to improve your mental golfing skills and thus make the utmost of your physical abilities. This is the lazy person's chapter of the busy person's golf book.

After all, thinking is the one area in which occasional golfers have as much natural talent as the pros do. You don't have to be a genius to be a great golfer. But if you want to stay out of trouble, if you want to make every shot count, if you want to achieve the best possible score you can without lots of practice, you have to do some smart thinking about every aspect of golf.

Unfortunately, most occasional golfers, from what I've seen, are careless thinkers. They set no goals for themselves. They don't think about each shot. They just aim in the direction of the green and hit. And when faced with a difficult decision they decide as much by emotion as by reason: "If I don't try to clear this lake, I'll look lily-livered." "If I try and fail, I'll look really stupid," and "Boy, wouldn't it be nice to have one to brag about in the clubhouse?"

Unfortunately, fuzzy thinking and emotional decision-making can be as costly as improper contact or an inconsistent swing. If you don't plan each shot carefully, you'll face difficulty in the shots that follow. If you don't realize when it's smart to gamble, you'll get into trouble and the strokes will multiply. And if you don't set goals for each round and compare your performance with those goals, you'll often end up scratching your head, wondering where you could have saved yourself some strokes. If, on the other hand, you learn to set realistic goals, plan each shot sensibly, and make careful decisions, you should drastically reduce your number of confrontations with quadruple bogeys. Careful planning and decision-making can lower your score.

Strategy for the occasional golfer is not exactly the same as strategy for the pro, because their skills differ. But their strategies are the same in one important respect: Sound strategy evolves from a firm knowledge of one's own abilities. The reason is that the better you know your abilities, the better you will be able to avoid your weaknesses.

This is the first important rule of smart golf thinking: Know your own abilities. There's a ditch 160 yards off the tee. Can you clear that ditch on the fly with your 3-wood? If you can, how often can you do it? If you hit a 3-iron to play short, what are the chances of your shot rolling into the ditch? What if you use a 5-iron? Knowing the answers to questions like these makes it much easier to make the right decision and stay out of trouble. Similar self-knowledge helps on every shot.

Knowing your own golfing plusses and minuses is so important that it's worth the trouble to take an inventory of them. So let's take a quiz. Get out paper and pencil and answer the following questions as truthfully as you can. Since this isn't a quiz to test how smart you are, there are no right answers. The only "right" answers are the honest answers, the honest answers about your own abilities.

1) What is your average score?
   What is your best score over the last year?
   What is your worst score over the last year?
2) On which holes do you lose the most strokes to par? On which holes do you come closest to par most often?
   par 3s, par 4s, par 5s

3) From the following list cross out any shots you never use. Then rank the remaining shots, starting with 1 for your strongest and best type of shot.

> tee shots with woods
> tee shots with irons
> fairway woods
> fairway shots with long irons (2, 3, 4)
> fairway shots with medium irons (5, 6)
> fairway shots with short irons (7, 8, 9)
> pitch shots
> chips
> sand shots
> putts

4) Rank the following shots in their order of difficulty for you.

> 150-yard 5-iron over a lake
> 120-yard 7-iron onto a 40 foot green
> 9-iron over a 60-foot tree 60 yards away
> 5-iron between two 40-foot trees 10 yards apart, 80 yards away

(In other words, which is easiest for you to achieve: Distance, placement, height or accuracy?)

5) On the average, how many putts do you take each round?

On the average, how many shots does it take you to get out of a trap?

What percentage of the time do you duff the ball from a bad lie?

How many holes per round do you usually score 3-over-par or worse?

When you've wasted shots, are you impatient about making them up?

Do you perform better under pressure, or worse?

Just thinking about these questions should give you a better idea of your own abilities and how well you know them. Were there any questions you couldn't answer? Better pay more attention as you play golf in the months ahead. In the meantime, keep in mind the answers you are sure of as you read the rest of this chapter.

Strategy, my dictionary says, is simply "a plan." Well, that's exactly what you, the occasional golfer, need. To cut down on your mistakes. To take advantage of strengths and avoid weaknesses. To motivate yourself. To help you concentrate. To clarify what you need to achieve on every shot. And to help you keep track of where those shots are piling up.

Where does planning begin? When, for example, do you begin to plan the tee shot you'll hit on the 18th hole? On the 18th tee? On the 17th hole? On the 9th? Actually, the groundwork for every single shot of a smart round of golf should be laid before the very first shot on the first hole. To know what you need to achieve on each shot you need to know what to achieve on each hole, and to know that you've got to have a plan for the entire round. That doesn't mean that before you pull your bag out of the trunk of your car you should decide what club you'll use on the 18th tee. But it does mean that if you want to achieve a certain score, you've got to think ahead.

Want to break 100? Okay, then make 99 your goal. Unless you're a beginner, 99 is not an unreasonable goal, especially if you've thoughtfully followed the advice in the previous chapters. What do you have to shoot on each hole to score 99? In terms of par, on a par-72 course 99 is 27 shots over par, or 1½ strokes a hole over par. One-and-a-half strokes a hole means that if you bogey 9 holes and double-bogey the other 9, you'll shoot a 99. So the trick is simply to decide which ones to try to bogey and which to double-bogey. This is where a knowledge of your abilities comes in. Do you come closer to par on par 3s, par 4s, or par 5s? If you are best on par 3s and worst on par 5s, then you should try to bogey the par 3s and double-bogey the 5s. If you hit long tee shots perhaps you'd aim for bogeys on the par 5s, double-bogeys on the par 3s. In either case, you'd probably try for bogeys on the short par 4s and double-bogeys on the long par 4s. If you have no preferences, you might try to bogey every hole, allowing yourself 9 extra shots for penalties and mistakes. Exactly how you divide up those 99 strokes is up to you. If you know the course well, you might want to make your allotments on the basis of factors other than distance, like traps, doglegs, lakes, and narrow fairways.

Whatever you decide, write your goal for each hole on your scorecard. Not only will this help you remember your scoring ambitions, but it will help you keep track of where you stand. If after the first nine you're four strokes over your goal you'll know to revamp your objectives for the back nine.

Be sure, however, that the goals you set are

realistic. Setting unrealistically difficult goals
will make you feel frustrated. If you aren't quite
ready to shoot for 99 try for 108, or all double-
bogeys. On the other hand, setting goals that are
too easy will only make you lazy and inattentive.
So if you've been averaging 95 why not aim for 90,
or all bogeys? In any case, it's important to set
goals for every round and every hole so that you
always know exactly what you have to achieve.
By getting in the habit of setting goals and trying
to reach them, you'll learn better concentration,
and lapses of attention will stop costing you
strokes.

Setting goals for each hole also helps you set
goals for each shot. Suppose, for example, that
the first hole is a long 440-yard par 4. Your
objective is a double-bogey 6. Now, how are you
going to achieve that? One drive, two fairway
irons, a chip, and two putts, and there's your 6.
Always allow for a chip and two putts. Allowing
less puts too much pressure on you around the
green, while allowing more than a chip and two
putts doesn't put you under enough. It's a good
habit to get into to try to get down in 3 strokes
whenever you are less than 75 yards away. Extra
chips and putts are frustrating and unnecessary.
They're just as costly as duffed drives, so do your
utmost to eliminate them.

Breaking the 6 strokes down even further, you
want to get close to the green in 3. A 160-yard
drive and two 130-yard fairway shots, for example, would put you within 20 yards of the green.
Those goals are fairly reasonable. So your goal on

the tee shot is simply to get 160 yards and stay out of trouble. You don't need a 200-yard drive on the first tee to be on your way to breaking 100. Just get a fair amount of distance on every shot. Even if there was a lake 160 yards from the tee, you could still get that double-bogey. A 140-yard drive and two 130-yard irons would put you within 40 yards of the green. The pros may reach the greens of long par 5s in 2, but you only need to be on the green in par.

The same advice applies to par 3s and 5s. On a 200-yard par-3 that you're trying to bogey, allow yourself a 160-yard tee shot, a 40-yard chip and two putts. On a 520-yard par 5 that you'd like to double-bogey, allow yourself a 160-yard drive, three 120-yard fairway irons, a chip from the fringe and two putts for a 7.

But what do you do when you duff a shot? Do you panic and try to make up for it immediately? Do you try to hit the ball out of a risky lie in the woods? Do you try to get 220 yards on your second shot? I can't stress this enough—on every shot you must set a reasonable goal for yourself. Don't try to make up the lost stroke with a fairway 2-wood and a prayer. If you try to accomplish the highly unlikely, all you're likely to be is highly unlucky. You'll probably tense up, overswing, and get into even worse trouble.

The thing to do if you've given a stroke away is to ask yourself, where can this stroke most reasonably be made up? In most cases you have three reasonable choices: Make it up gradually, make it up around the green, or make it up on another hole. Let's say on that 440-yard hole you hit your tee shot 100 yards instead of the desired 160. You've got 60 yards to make up. Instead of trying to get those yards back immediately, plan on getting them back gradually. Get 20 on the next shot, 20 on the one after that, and plan on chipping onto the green from 40 instead of 20 yards out. That's not unreasonable. But if that doesn't work out, you can still try the second strategy: making it up around the green. Remember how you planned on 2-putting this hole? Well, you've still got a chance to chip close enough to one-putt. After all, with that extra 100 yards you should be nearly on the fringe of the green in four strokes. From there you've got a real shot at eliminating a putt.

If that doesn't work, and you triple-bogey the hole, you still have the third strategy: Make it up on another hole. Look over your scorecard. Which hole has the easiest goal for you to achieve? The 100-yard par-3 you planned to bogey? The 380-yard par-4 you planned to double-bogey? The 500-yard par-5 you planned to double-bogey? Pick the one that's easiest and subtract one shot from your goal for that hole. Then concentrate on your original plans for the next hole and forget the lost shot until later.

Suppose, however, you hit a 190-yard tee shot on that first hole. Does that mean you should try to hit your second shot only 100 yards? Of course not. If 130 yards was a reasonable goal for a second shot before, it's still reasonable. Goals should not only be reasonable, they should also be effective. Abandon your plans whenever you can surpass them. After all, unless you've included some leeway in your plans, you're going to have to balance each goal you fail to achieve by surpassing another.

The smart golfer, however, considers more factors in planning each shot than just distance. Location is crucial. On every shot the smart golfer thinks, does it matter where this ball lands? Often, by asking yourself this question, you can avoid a lot of later trouble. See that 80-foot oak out there on your right? Do you really want that in your way on your second shot? Notice how the lake is much narrower on the left? Wouldn't it be much safer, then, to try to clear it from the left on your second shot? Do you see how there are traps in front of the green and on the left side? Although you can't reach them, do you really want to hit over them on your next shot? Notice how the green slopes quickly downhill 6 feet beyond the cup? Wouldn't you rather then hit your 30-foot putt a little short than a little long? Always think: What's the best place to be to stay out of trouble, to give me the easiest next shot, and to give me the best aproach to the green? Remember an extra chip or an unnecessary putt is just as costly as a duffed drive.

Consider the lie you'll have if you reach your destination. If the area is muddy or rocky or downhill, are you sure you want to hit there? You shouldn't, if there's some flat, fluffy fairway that's just as easy to reach. And consider that it's

4. PLAN EACH HOLE

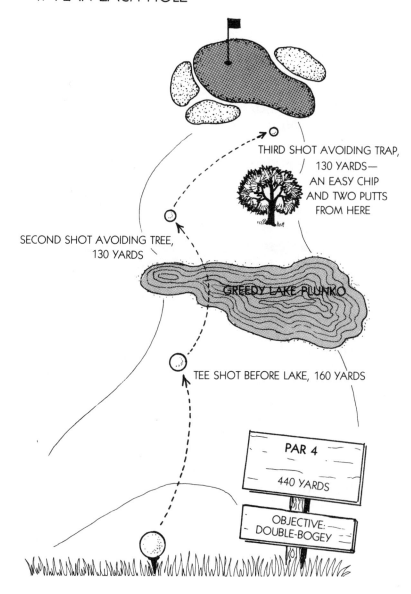

THIRD SHOT AVOIDING TRAP, 130 YARDS— AN EASY CHIP AND TWO PUTTS FROM HERE

SECOND SHOT AVOIDING TREE, 130 YARDS

GREEDY LAKE PLUNKO

TEE SHOT BEFORE LAKE, 160 YARDS

PAR 4

440 YARDS

OBJECTIVE: DOUBLE-BOGEY

probably better to have a tough shot from a good lie than a shot without obstacles from a bad one. But you're the best judge of how well you hit from bad lies, so you be the judge.

No less important is visualizing how a shot will land and roll. How is the ball going to bounce on that downhill slope near the lake? Is your chip going to break towards the hole or away from it when the ball reaches the green? Wouldn't it be a shame to hit a solid shot and then to see your ball bounce and bounce and bounce into oblivion in the lake? And wouldn't it be embarrassing to hit a nice chip onto the green, only to see the ball roll and roll downhill into a trap? So think about the consequences of every shot—the landing, the lie, and the location. This habit will save you needless strokes several times every round. Foresight beats hindsight. When you have the consequences clear in your mind, you'll usually know the right decision to make, the wise shot to attempt. But that's not always true.

Tricky decisions do crop up. You might find yourself faced with a risky shot that could save you a stroke, or even two, if you could bring it off. Such shots can be very tempting, especially if you've had a bad round so far and would like to have at least one shot to be proud of in the clubhouse. On the other hand, the risks might backfire and cost even more strokes than you might have saved. When faced with temptation, what do you do? Do you challenge obstacles or avoid them? Do you aim for the safe spot or gamble? This question is extremely important, for not knowing how to gamble is one of the costliest problems of the occasional golfer.

Let's take three situations. In the first, a 70-foot sycamore guards the corner of a dogleg. If you hit over it, you could save yourself a stroke, because it would take you two shots to reach the same spot by going around it. On the other hand, going over the tree is risky. If you don't make it, you could ricochet off into the woods or even bounce right back where you were. Going around the tree, however, is perfectly safe. The fairway is wide open and there are no traps or water hazards to worry about.

In the second situation, there is a lake 160 yards off the tee. You know you have the ability to clear the lake if you hit a good shot. If you don't make it, however, you'll lose the ball and gain a penalty stroke. On the other hand, hitting short and then over is reasonably easy.

In situation three, the flagstick is placed on the right side of the green, close to several traps—one to the right, one in front, one in back. The left side of the green is wide open with no traps; it's safe. You're 60 yards away. If you could put the ball on the green near the hole, you might save a stroke. But you also might end up in a trap. If you aim to the left, you'd have little chance for a 1-putt, but only a terrible shot could get you into trouble.

What do you do?

Almost all occasional golfers, if they are serious about their scores, should choose the safe

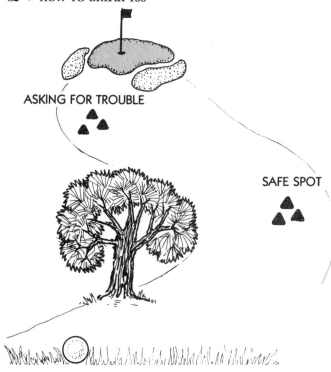

ASKING FOR TROUBLE

SAFE SPOT

spot. Don't try to clear the tree, don't challenge the lake, don't go for the pin. Go around, play short, hit to the open area, play for security. Penalty strokes can sabotage your score. Many golfers can't break 100, not because they don't have the ability to get bogeys, but because they score too many 9s and 10s by getting into trouble and staying there. The simple truth is that problems have a way of multiplying. If the ball goes into the woods, it'll cost you another stroke to get it out. If the ball bounces back to you, you face the same choices all over again. And, having lost a stroke, are you likely to play it safe the second time? If you don't, you could still end up in the woods, and need 4 more strokes to get to that spot on the other side of the tree.

Take trying to clear the lake. If you don't make it, you might be tempted to try it again so that

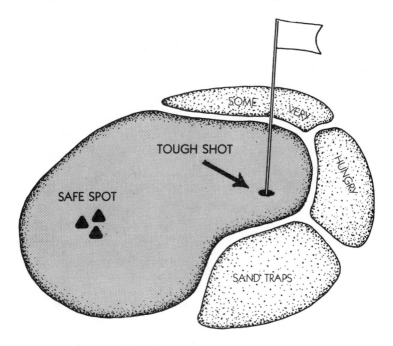

you lie 2 on the other side instead of 2 on this side. Plunk, in goes another one. Do you try for 3? How many times have you seen somebody hit 3 shots into a lake? I've seen it many times. It's not all that uncommon.

Take aiming for the flagstick on that well-trapped hole. If you don't make it, you're in the sand. Can you plan sand shots well? If not, you may be back in the sand after one try getting out, or you may hit out of the sand only to wind up knocking the ball onto the left side of the green, the very safe spot you might have tried for in the first place.

In general, occasional golfers should aim for the safe spots. The big difference between a safe shot and a gamble is that on a gamble you stand a good chance of ending up worse off than you were when you started. You may lose a fantasy stroke by playing it safe, but you can lose several real ones by gambling. After all, mistakes make golfers upset, and upset golfers are prone to make even more mistakes.

Some golfers, however, may be reluctant to accept this advice. It's not as exciting to play it safe. It's not as much of a challenge, they think. And it's giving up the chance for that spectacular shot. But just as you should give up trying to "kill it with a big backswing," you should give up trying to bet when the cards are stacked against you if you're serious about lowering your score. Besides, it's a far more difficult challenge to play consistently good golf than to get lucky, and the satisfaction of lowering your score can more than outweigh the fleeting excitement of the luckiest shot.

This is in no way to say, however, that there is never a time and place for gambling on the golf course. Of course there is. Remember the quiz question, "Which is the easiest for you to achieve: distance, placement, height, or accuracy?" That was asked to help you pinpoint your gambling strengths.

If you can get consistent distance, then you might regularly try to clear ponds and streams and other hazards. If you have an ability to judge distances and place the ball, you might go for the flag that's bounded by bunkers. If you can consistently get height on your shots, you might consider trying to go over tall trees sometimes. Or, if you're accurate, you might try to hit a shot between two tall trees, or to cut a dogleg closely. In every case the rule is: If you must gamble, gamble on your strengths, never on your weaknesses.

A further caution: If there are several difficulty factors, don't gamble. If you need height *and* you have a bad lie, play it safe. If you need both accuracy *and* distance—say, a long shot to a green bordered by traps—play it safe. The odds are not in your favor. Gamble only on simple shots that depend on your strengths.

In fact, any schemes you can concoct for taking advantage of your strengths and avoiding your weaknesses will save you strokes. Are you horrendous at getting out of traps? Then do your best to avoid them when you play (and your best to confront them if you practice). If you can't hit a wood off a tee, don't worry about being embarrassed, use an iron. If you can't putt well, concentrate on chipping as close as you can. Steer to your strength.

Another suggestion is to play the "hot" clubs. Suppose you notice that you're hitting exceptionally good 5-irons one day. Then stick with that 5-iron whenever you reasonably can. On the other hand, suppose you're struggling with your trusty old 2-wood off the tee. Then you might try teeing off with your 3, staying with it if it works. Any day you find one club is unreliable, spurn that cold club and grab another. You may find a hot club.

A couple of final remarks about strategy. Take advantage of course conditions. If the traps are filled with water, try to stay out. But if they're so hard the ball will bounce out of them, why not challenge them? If the wind is in your face, don't try to clear the lake. But if it's behind you, your chances are improved. And, of course, if the lake is frozen over, go for it.

Finally, learn from your mistakes and successes. At the end of every round look at your scorecard and think back on your performance. Learn more about your own abilities and limitations. Try to find out something about your strengths and weaknesses that you can use the next time you play. A couple of minutes of thinking can often be as valuable as a half-hour of practice to the golfer who's been struggling to average under 100.

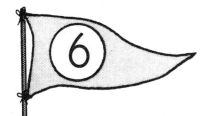

How to make the most of a little practice

If you don't spend much time practicing, it's crucial to use the time you do spend wisely. Most golfers spend their practice time trying to crush 1-woods off rubber tees or attempting 30-footers on the practice green for five minutes before the start of a round. What a waste of time! No wonder they don't improve. What good is swinging with all your might if you're not going to swing that way out on the course? What good is hitting from a rubber tee if the ball doesn't sit that high on a regular tee? What good is attempting a 30-foot putt, when it's the missed 6-footers that really cost you strokes?

There are two keys to making the most of your practice time: 1) Simulate game conditions, and 2) Work on your weaknesses first. Simulating game conditions means re-creating, in practice, exactly the same situations you'll face out on the golf course. Since the object of practice is to improve your ability to perform on the course, doesn't it make sense to swing just the way you swing on the course? Shouldn't you place the ball the way it'll be placed on the course? Shouldn't you practice with various clubs since you'll use all of them out on the course? And shouldn't you work on accuracy and placement as well as distance when they are so important in actual play?

One by one, let's discuss the various aspects of simulating game conditions.

Equipment: Practice with the same equipment you use when you play, if you can. Take your own clubs if you go to the driving range. Don't use their old woods or borrow clubs from a friend. And don't even bother to take along clubs you own but never use. If you only practice a little, it's very important to become as accustomed as you can to the feel of the clubs you're in the habit of using. You may not realize it, but every time you swing an unfamiliar club you're not only missing an opportunity to master the familiar club, you're also developing a feel for the wrong club and can wind up hurting your game.

Next, practice with real golf balls, not plastic ones, when you can. Practicing with plastic golf balls just isn't the same as practicing with the genuine article. You can feel a club turn in your hands at impact with a Wilson; you can't with a Whiffle. You can tell from the trajectory and the sound when you've stroked a Royal royally; you can't with a polyethylene. Since you do get *some* feel for your swing, however, it's probably better to practice with plastic golf balls than not to practice at all.

Finally, the clothes you wear when you practice should be similar to the clothes you wear when you play. If you practice in a three-piece suit and street shoes, you're not going to be able to swing in your regular pattern. The same applies to wearing a bathing suit and sandals. So dress for practice the same way you dress for play. If you play wearing a golf glove, wear it when you practice. If you play wearing golf spikes, then wear them, if you can, during practice.

The Lie: When practicing, play the ball the way you would play it out on the course. Hitting from a rubber tee in a rubber mat just isn't the same as hitting from a wooden tee in the grass. Rubber tees are often too high, and clubs that will dig into grass simply bounce off the rubber mats. So, if you can, find a grassy area and hit from wooden tees. Similarly, hitting from mats of plastic "grass" is just not the same as hitting from the real thing. Again, the ball sits up too high and the club won't dig in with plastic grass. So hit practice irons from true turf, and make an effort to put the ball on thin grass or even dirt, so you'll be prepared for difficult lies when you go out on the course. The same principles apply to putting and sand shots. Putting on a green is best, although putting on carpet can be better than not practicing at all. But sand shots, to be of any real value, must be hit from the sand, even from slightly buried lies in the sand. Hitting sand wedges from the grass just can't teach you how to get out of traps.

The Swing: Practice swinging the same way you swing on the course. Don't try to kill the ball. Don't clown around for your friends. Don't "just try" different grips, stances, backswings, rhythms, or follow-throughs. If you have a problem and you have the time to work on it, fine. You should work on it. But if you're comfortable with your swing or you don't have time for an overhaul, practice the swing you'll be using out on the course. Improve your feel for the real thing if you want more consistency and control in your swing.

The Club: Every club you use on the course is a club you should think about practicing with. It's amazing how many golfers never practice with some of their clubs. Some only practice with woods, some only practice with irons, some only practice putting. If you're serious about making the most of your practice time, try to practice with all of your clubs. This doesn't mean you have to practice with each and every club every time you work on your game. Over the course of several practice sessions, however, you should practice a little with all of your clubs.

At the same time, don't practice with clubs you don't use. If you don't use a 1-wood, a 2-iron, or a pitching wedge, leave them at home in the closet. If you're going to devote lots of time to learning how to use them, fine. But don't waste your time with clubs you'll never use.

The Shot: Practice the shots you'll use on the course. Every round of golf involves chipping, putting, fairway irons, sand shots, and tee shots. So if you want to improve, you should practice all these shots. That doesn't mean you have to practice them all every time you practice. And it doesn't mean you have to practice more often. But you shouldn't neglect any one type of shot. They're all important. So try to work on each type of shot over several practice sessions. If you worked on tee shots last week, practice your chipping this week. If you worked on putting last month, practice getting out of sand this month.

Of course, except for tee shots and putts, it's not always easy to find places to practice certain golf shots. Many driving ranges, however, do have grassy patches where you can hit irons. Some even have sand traps you can use, but you might have to do some hunting around. You could practice chipping on the empty football field down the road or practice your sand shots on a beach. But since it's best to practice just before you play, you might look around for a way to practice at the course itself. Is anyone on the 18th hole? If not, you might toss a few in the trap and try to get out. Or you might sneak in some practice shots while you're playing. If no one's behind you and your partners don't mind, you might hit a few extra chips or sand shots for practice. You just might play 9 holes some deserted Tuesday instead of going to the driving range, rehitting any shots you botch. Chip-and-putt courses are also a way to practice the all-important shots around the green. The pros work on all their shots by playing all the time. For golfers who can't afford the time or the money to play several times a week, being resourceful in finding ways to practice is especially important.

Finally, practice the type of shots you're most likely to see on the course. Don't practice 50-foot putts with crazy breaks. Practice the 6-footers you see all the time. Don't hit just buried sand shots. First master the easy ones you see more often.

Objectives: In practice, try to accomplish the same objectives you'd try to accomplish out on the course. For example, don't just hit 7-irons without concern for direction or placement. On the course you'll try to land 7-iron shots on greens. So in practice, pick a spot and try to land on it. Imagine it's a green. Work on accuracy. Work on placement. Work on your judgment of distances. By concentrating on controlling your shots, you'll be surprised how quickly your control can improve. And, of course, any improvement in your control and consistency should translate itself immediately into a lower score.

The Check-it Swing: You do take a Check-it swing before almost every shot on the course, don't you? Then use it in practice. After all, making proper contact is important in practice too.

Attitude: Out on the golf course you take every shot seriously. Do the same in practice. Treat every shot as if it's important. Plan each shot. Concentrate. Pretend you're under pressure. If you don't hit this ball solidly, it'll drop in the lake. If you make this putt, you'll break 100. You *play* under pressure, so *practice* under pressure. This habit will help you concentrate when you practice.

In short, if you really want to make the most of your practice time, do everything you can to simulate game situations. Practice with the same conditions, equipment, frame of mind, goals, swing, and shots that you'll be involved with out on the course. The closer you duplicate course conditions, the more likely your practicing is to improve your score.

The second key to getting more out of practice sessions is to work on your weaknesses first. These weaknesses are causing strokes to pile up. It is the area where practicing will do you the most good because it's where there is the most room for improvement. There is no surer way to lower your score than to turn what was a liability into a strength. Conversely, there is no better way to get negligible returns than to work on what you are already good at. Unfortunately, a lot of occasional golfers work on their strengths in practice, trying to coax every inch they can out of their tee shots or trying to hole out wandering 50-foot putts. But what good does it do you to get 10 more yards out of your woods if it still takes you 2 shots to get out of a sand trap? And what good does it do to consistently 2-putt from 60 feet if you can't get 60 yards with a fairway iron? If you want to make the most of your practice time, if you want to do your best to improve your score and your skills, give practicing priority to your weaknesses to eliminate the areas in which you're piling those strokes.

Understand, however, that working on weaknesses does not mean working on difficult shots you don't need. You don't need a 1-wood, a 2-iron or pitching wedge to shoot in the 90s or even the 80s. You don't need to learn to intentionally fade or hook. You don't need to hit woods from fairways or long irons out of fairway traps. But you do need to putt well, get out of sand traps in one stroke, chip near the hole from the fringe of the green, land on greens from within 100 yards, hit 5-irons from fairways, and to hit 3-woods from tees. If you can't consistently accomplish one of these shots, put it at the top of your list to work on the next time you practice. It has to be costing you many unnecessary strokes. But don't worry about difficult, fancy shots you don't really need.

Work on your weaknesses and simulate game conditions. If you can practice only a little, make it count.

But, of course, even if you don't practice at all, you can still break 100. Just remember the shortcuts the pros don't tell you.